BUILDING ON A FIRM FOUNDATION

Faith One Publishing
7901 S. Vermont, Los Angeles, CA 90044

life without meaning
becomes miserable

Maal

BUILDING
ON A FIRM
FOUNDATION
A Guide to Developing
Your Christian Walk

by
Frederick K.C. Price, D.D.

FAITH ONE
PUBLISHING

Building on a Firm Foundation
ISBN 1-883798-21-3
Copyright © 1998 by
Frederick K.C. Price, D.D.
P.O. Box 90000
Los Angeles, CA 90009

Published by Faith One Publishing
7901 South Vermont Avenue
Los Angeles, CA 90044

Contents

Introduction

At the time I discovered that the Word of God — the Holy Bible — was the Believer's guide to successful Christian living, my finances were in a shambles. I could not adequately provide for my family; I was sick and I felt defeated, even though I was saved and functioning in the office of pastor.

After years of studying the Bible and applying its life-changing principles to the circumstances of life, I learned what it means to **walk by faith and not by sight** (2 Corinthians 5:7) and how to achieve prosperity of spirit, soul, body, and finances by acting on God's Word. I learned that the Word works, and because God is not a respecter of persons (Acts 10:34), His Word can work in your life, as well.

Toward this end, I have developed this book as a guide to help the new Believer get started on a life-long journey leading to success and prosperity as a follower of Jesus Christ. Even if you have not yet been exposed to the basic teachings of Christianity, I believe you will receive a measure of blessing from what is contained in this book.

I encourage you to start with the beginning-understanding the gift of **salvation.** Advance on to the **Holy Spirit** and the importance of speaking with other tongues. Finally, continue on through the **principles of faith.** No teaching of the full Gospel, as recorded in the New Testament, would be complete with- out instructions on divine healing and finan- cial prosperity. It is God's will that His chil- dren prosper in **all** things and be in health, just as their souls prosper (3 John 2).

Take each chapter in this book and diligently study it. Look up the scriptures given at the end of the chapter, and of course, apply what you read to your life. By doing these things, you will be **building on a firm foundation** for success -spirit, soul, and body.

Frederick K.C. Price

1

Salvation — And What It Means for the Believer

In Job 14:14, Job asks, "If a man dies, shall he live again?" This question is essential to every human being. One answer is found in John 11:25-26. In this passage of Scripture, Jesus is responding to a statement made by Martha, one of the sisters of Lazarus. Lazarus was a dear friend of Jesus who had recently died, and Martha was saying that if Jesus had been there, her brother would not have died.

> Jesus said to her, "I am the resurrection and the life. He who believes in Me, though he may die, he shall live.
> "And whoever lives and believes in Me shall never die...."

What is crucial to understand here is that Jesus is not talking about natural or physical death. He uses this opportunity to state a profound truth that is the underlying fabric of all Christianity — that a person is either spiritually ALIVE or spiritually DEAD according to whether or not the person established a relationship with Christ while he or she was physically alive.

What It Means to be Spiritually Alive

When a person confesses (accepts or receives) Jesus as Savior and Lord, this person is deemed to have experienced the new birth. He or she is now alive to God in Christ Jesus (1 Corinthians 15:22). This person is then said to be born again (John 3:3), saved (Romans 10:9-10), a child of God (John 1:12), or a Christian (1 Peter 4:16).

The opposite of saved, of course, is lost. Therefore, anyone who does not accept, or receive, or confess Jesus as Savior and Lord is considered a non-Christian, a non-Believer, unsaved, and condemned (John 3:16-18). But the Word tells us in 2 Peter 3:9 that God is **not**

willing that any should perish, but that all
should come to repentance.

Why It Is Necessary to Confess Jesus to Be Saved

When God created the Earth, He invested
the totality of mankind in the first man,
Adam. God gave Adam dominion over the
earth and all that was in it (Genesis 1:26).
The devil, in the form of a serpent, tempted
Adam's mate, Eve, to eat of the fruit of the
tree that God had commanded Adam not to
eat. She succumbed to this temptation, and
when she offered the fruit to Adam, he also
ate of it.

In this act of disobedience, Adam rejected
God's lordship over him. In effect, he put
himself and his mate under the dominion of
Satan. Because Adam represented all of
mankind, this meant that all mankind would
come under the dominion of Satan, and their
rulership of the Earth passed to him.

3

Spiritual Versus Natural Death

Losing dominion over the Earth was not the most tragic result of Adam's transgression against God. The most tragic consequence was that Satan's rebellious nature, called the "sin nature," became a part of man's nature. The sin nature spiritually separated mankind from God. This spiritual separation is called *spiritual death.*

When most people think of the word *death,* they think of the end of existence. This is how we have been conditioned to think of death in our society. But when the Bible talks about spiritual death, it is talking about something totally different. It is talking about being "cut off" or not in right standing with God. When you are spiritually dead, you still exist as a spirit person, living in a physical body. However, you exist separate and apart from the life and nature of God.

What constitutes physical death is your spirit and soul separating from your body. This is when you physically die. But your spirit and soul continue living. The body is buried or burned (as in the case of cremation) and returns to dust. The spirit and soul either ascend to heaven or descend to hell, depending on whether the person established a relationship with Christ while he or she was physically alive.

God's Solution for Man's Condition

God is so good, and loves you and me so much, that even though Adam disobeyed Him, He did something about spiritual death so that we could escape it. That "something" is really a "someone" — His Son, the Lord Jesus Christ.

Jesus came to Earth in human form. Through His death, burial, and resurrection, He provided the redemption necessary for mankind to enjoy the father-child relationship that had existed with Almighty God before Adam's sin. There was, however, one added stipulation. Every person, upon reaching the age of accountability, must now choose between having God as his spiritual Father (by accepting Jesus as Savior and Lord), or having Satan as his spiritual head (by rejecting Jesus, whether or not the person realizes the choice he has made by his rejection). The age of accountability can differ in chronological age for each individual. Nevertheless, every individual who is given the opportunity to accept Jesus as Lord and Savior has a critical and lasting choice to make.

In Acts 4:12, the Apostle Peter says this about the Lord Jesus Christ:

> **"Nor is there salvation in any other, for there is no other name under heaven given among men by which we must be saved."**

And Jesus said in John 14:6, speaking about Himself:

> **"I am the way, the truth, and the life. No one comes to the Father except through Me."**

From these two verses alone, one can see that Jesus is God's only way for man to be saved and, thereby, become spiritually alive.

Passing From Death to Life

Jesus said in John 5:24:

> **"Most assuredly, I say to you, he who hears My word and believes in Him who sent Me has everlasting life, and shall not come into judgment, BUT HAS PASSED FROM DEATH INTO LIFE."**

Normally, the cycle is to go from life to death. So what is Jesus talking about here?

Every person who comes into this world inherits his or her parents' sin nature. They received this nature from their parents, who got it from their parents, and so on down the line, all the way back to Adam and Eve. This nature is a spiritually dead nature. This is why the Bible says we move **"from death into life"** when we accept Jesus as our personal Savior and Lord.

Notice the phrase, **"But HAS passed from death into life."** *Has* is past-tense; it shows that an action has already taken place. This means that the moment a person confesses Jesus as Savior and Lord, he or she immediately becomes the possessor of eternal life. This

7

person passes from death into everlasting life, and receives right standing with God.

Neither water baptism, church membership, confirmation, nor anything else can bring a man into a state of salvation. Only receiving Jesus as Savior can do this.

Everything Jesus did from the cross to the grave, He did on man's behalf as our substitute. When He died, we died; when He arose from the dead, we arose from the dead; and when He defeated Satan in the pit of hell, we defeated Satan. Jesus bought back for mankind everlasting redemption. He also made it possible for us to be overcomers in every situation of life through the operation of faith in the Bible as the Word of God (2 Timothy 3:16-17).

Being born again, or saved, is the most important thing in your life. You should know whether you are saved as well as you know your own name. If you are not sure about your salvation, I urge you to stop right now and clear this matter up. Ask Jesus to come into your heart. Don't let another minute go by!

Prayer for Salvation

Dear God,

    I come to You with a humble heart and with gratitude for sending Your Son Jesus Christ to take away my sin that I might have right-standing with You.

    I accept Jesus now as my Savior and Lord, and I turn from my past life to a renewed life in You through Him.

    Dear heavenly Father, I thank You now for accepting me as Your child. You said in Your Word that if I confess with my mouth the Lord Jesus and believe in my heart that God raised Him from the dead, I would be saved (Romans 10:9). I have just made this confession. I believe Your Word; I believe that I am now saved and I thank You for the gift of salvation and for accepting me as Your child. In Jesus' Name, Amen.

Reference Scriptures

Romans 5:12	Ephesians 2:1-5
Romans 3:23	John 20:31
John 3:16	Ephesians 2:8-9
Romans 10:9-10	Romans 3:10-12
John 1:12	John 16:30-31
Acts 4:12	Acts 10:43

If for some reason, after you have confessed Jesus as Savior and Lord, you still have some doubts about your salvation, the following scriptures should minister to you:

2 Corinthians 5:7	1 John 4:15
Romans 10:9-10	1 John 5:11-13
1 John 1:9	

The following scriptures will help you to know or help you to be assured of your salvation:

2 Corinthians 5:7	2 Corinthians 3:16-17
2 Corinthians 6:14-16	1 Corinthians 6:19-20
Romans 8:37	Galatians 4:7
Galatians 3:26-29	Ephesians 2:6
Ephesians 1:19-23	

2
The Holy Spirit and What It Means to Speak With Other Tongues

In Mark 16:17, Jesus states:

> **"And these signs will follow those who believe: In My name they will cast out demons; they will speak with new tongues."**

Jesus says, **"And these signs will follow those who believe."** He does not say these signs will follow only the females who believe, or only the males who believe. He says these signs will follow **those who believe.** In other words, these signs will follow those Believers who believe these signs will follow what they do in Jesus' name.

One of the signs Jesus mentions is speaking with new tongues. The Greek word translated as *tongues* in Mark 16:17 is *glossa*, which means "languages." Some people read this verse and

11

think it means that if you used foul language before you were saved, you will automatically stop using it once you are saved. But this is not what Jesus is saying here.

Jesus is saying that if you are a Believer, and you believe that these signs will follow, you will speak with new languages. In fact, speaking with tongues is the biblical sign or evidence for being filled with the Holy Spirit.

Acts 2:1-4:

> **When the Day of Pentecost had fully come, they were all with one accord in one place.**
> **And suddenly there came a sound from heaven, as of a rushing mighty wind, and it filled the whole house where they were sitting.**
> **Then there appeared to them divided tongues, as of fire, and one sat upon each of them.**
> **And they were all filled with the Holy Spirit and began to speak with other tongues, as the Spirit gave them utterance.**

Tongues in verse four is the word *glossa*, the same word used in Mark 16:17. We could paraphrase Acts 2:4 this way: "And they were all filled with the Holy Spirit and began to speak in other languages supernaturally...."

Acts 10:44-46:

> While Peter was still speaking these words, the Holy Spirit fell upon all those who heard the word.
> And those of the circumcision who believed were astonished, as many as came with Peter, because the gift of the Holy Spirit had been poured out on the Gentiles also.
> For they heard them speak with tongues and magnify God....

Acts 19:1-2:

> And it happened, while Apollos was at Corinth, that Paul, having passed through the upper regions, came to Ephesus. And finding some disciples/
> he said to them, "Did you receive the Holy Spirit when you believed?" So they said to him, "We have not so much as heard whether there is a Holy Spirit."

Some people have the misconception that being born again and being filled with the Holy Spirit is the same transaction. However, Paul asked the disciples in Ephesus, **"Did you receive the Holy Spirit when you believed?"** (In this instance, I prefer the traditional King James Version of Acts 19:2, which states, "... Have ye received the Holy Ghost since ye believed?") If anyone would know whether getting saved meant being filled with the Holy Spirit, it would be Paul.

Acts 19:3-6:

> **And he said to them, "Into what then were you baptized?" So they said, "Into John's baptism."**
>
> **Then Paul said, "John indeed baptized with a baptism of repentance, saying to the people that they should believe on Him who would come after him, that is, on Christ Jesus."**
>
> **When they heard this, they were baptized in the name of the Lord Jesus.**
>
> **And when Paul had laid hands on them, the Holy Spirit came upon them, and they spoke with tongues and prophesied.**

Again, the word *tongues* in verse six is *glossa*, meaning "languages" — not one, but many. They spoke with tongues other than their native languages.

Is Speaking With Tongues the Gift of Tongues?

One point of confusion for many people is that they lump speaking with tongues together with the gift of different kinds of tongues (called "divers kinds of tongues" in the King James Version of the Bible). Again, in Mark 16:17, Jesus tells us:

"And these signs will follow those who believe: In My name they will cast out demons; they will speak with new tongues."

Jesus says that the signs will follow those who believe. So, if you are a Believer, these signs should follow you. In other words, you should be a believing Believer, rather than an unbelieving Believer who remains sick, poor, whipped and defeated in life!

When it comes to the gift of tongues, Paul says this in 1 Corinthians 12:7-11:

But the manifestation of the Spirit is given to each one for the profit of all: for to one is given the word of wisdom through the Spirit, to another the word of knowledge through the same Spirit, to another faith

by the same Spirit, to another gifts of healings by the same Spirit, to another the working of miracles, to another prophecy, to another discerning of spirits, to another different kinds of tongues, to another the interpretation of tongues.

But one and the same Spirit works all these things, distributing to each one individually as He wills.

Notice, all of these spiritual gifts are given to individuals, not to every Christian. This must mean then that the gift of different or divers kinds of tongues is not the same as what you speak when you are filled with the Spirit. Paul is talking about the supernatural manifestations of the gifts of the Spirit. Not every Christian will have these manifestations, but everyone who is filled with the Holy Spirit can and should speak with new tongues.

Some people use 1 Corinthians 12:7-11 to prove that not everyone can speak with other tongues. But as I said before, Paul is not talking in this passage about the infilling of the Holy Spirit. He is talking about the spiritual gifts which manifest as the Holy Spirit wills to edify the corporate Body of Christ. (Note: Any and everyone who operates in these spiritual gifts MUST first be filled with the Holy Spirit according to Acts 2:4.)

Another passage that is used to "prove" that not everyone will speak with other tongues when they are filled with the Spirit is 1 Corinthians 12:28-30:

> **And God has appointed these in the church: first apostles, second prophets, third teachers, after that miracles, then gifts of healings, helps, administrations, varieties of tongues.**
> **Are all apostles? Are all prophets? Are all teachers? Are all workers of miracles?**
> **Do all have gifts of healings? Do all speak with tongues? Do all interpret?**

In this passage and in Ephesians 4:11-13, Paul talks about apostles, prophets, evangelists, pastors and teachers. These are not spiritual gifts. They are ministry gifts God has set in the Church to edify the Body of Christ for the work of the ministry, as well as to perfect the saints. These gifts are people, not supernatural manifestations of the Holy Spirit.

The only difference between the list above and the one in Ephesians is that, in 1 Corinthians, Paul lists only three of the five ministry offices by their categorical names. He lists the other two offices by their functional names — in other words, by the spiritual gifts that should be functioning in their ministries. The working of miracles and gifts of healings should operate in the ministry of the evangelist. The term *administrations* relates to the office of pastor, because the pastor is the head of the local church.

Paul asks in 1 Corinthians 12:29-30, **Are all apostles? Are all prophets? Are all teachers? Are all workers of miracles? Do all have gifts of healings? Do all speak with tongues? Do all interpret?** The answer to all of these questions is, of course not. Not every Christian is called to one of the five-fold ministry gifts, and the ministry gifts are what are discussed here.

Benefits

First Corinthians 14 lists several reasons we should speak with new tongues.

1 Corinthians 14:2:

> **For he who speaks in a tongue does not speak to men but to God, for no one understands him; however, in the spirit he speaks mysteries.**

A better translation for the word *mysteries* in the Greek would be *divine secrets*. In the latter part of this verse, Paul states, **... for no one understands him; however, in the spirit....** In John 4:24, Jesus says, **"God is Spirit, and those who worship Him must worship in spirit and truth."** Paul adds in Hebrews 12:9:

> **Furthermore, we have had human fathers who corrected us, and we paid them respect. Shall we not much more readily be in subjection to the Father of spirits and live?**

The word *spirits* is in small case, which means Paul is talking about the spirit of man. God is not the Father of your flesh and blood. God is the Father of you, and you are a spirit.

You may have heard people say, "Well, I'm just flesh and blood. What do you expect?" But this statement is not really true. You are a spirit, and you live inside of a flesh-and-blood body. You are not flesh and blood. In fact, there is an easy way to prove this. All you have to do is go to the cemetery, unearth some caskets, and see how many live bodies you run into. What made those bodies alive were the spirits that lived inside of them.

Let me give you another illustration. When I am wearing a suit of clothes, my suit moves with my movements. It is, in effect, "alive" because I am wearing it. However, when I take off my suit, it no longer moves or is "alive" because I am no longer wearing it. Your physical body is your "earth suit." When you "wear" or inhabit it, it allows you to live in this three-dimensional, physical realm. However, the real you is a spirit. You inhabit your physical body and give it life.

Now, your Father has devised a method by which your spirit can talk to Him as a spirit without your flesh getting in the way. This can be very desirable, because sometimes our flesh gets in the way. Sometimes our heads get in the way. Our minds, the soul part of us, messes us up in many areas. Speaking with

20

tongues is how our spirits can talk with God without the influence of our souls or bodies.

Paul states another benefit of speaking with tongues in 1 Corinthians 14:4: **He who speaks in a tongue edifies himself....** The word in English that best corresponds to what Paul says here is *charge*, as in charging a battery. God has given us a way to keep our spiritual batteries charged up so we can stay spiritually strong.

Another verse that talks about charging ourselves up is Jude 20:

> **But you, beloved, building yourselves up on your most holy faith, praying in the Holy Spirit.**

Build up in this verse means the same as to "charge up." You pray in the Holy Spirit by praying with other tongues. However, notice what Jude does not say. He does not say that praying in the Holy Spirit will *give you* faith. He says it will *build you up on your most holy faith*. You already have faith if you are born-again. However, praying in the Holy Spirit will build you up on this faith.

21

Letting Your Spirit Pray

In the first part of 1 Corinthians 14:14, Paul tells us, **For if I pray in a tongue, my spirit prays....** Speaking with tongues is actually prayer. According to this verse, if you do not pray in a tongue, your spirit does not pray. Your understanding is your mind. Your mind is located in the soul part of your three-fold nature, along with your will, your desire, and your emotions — in other words, your personality.

1 Corinthians 14:15:

> **What is the conclusion then? I will pray with the spirit, and I will also pray with the understanding. I will sing with the spirit, and I will also sing with the understanding.**

You can pray both with your spirit and with your understanding. Sometimes you want to pray with your understanding. For example, if we are getting ready to eat some food, and I am going to pray over it, I want you to be in agreement with me. In this case, I need to pray with the understanding so you can agree with me. But if I want to edify myself, I pray with my spirit.

In essence, speaking with tongues is a hot line to heaven. It is a line the devil cannot tap into (which is why he has spent so much time and effort to scare, goad, and reason people out of it). It is also a language not limited by vocabulary or education, so you can fully express yourself to the Father.

For example, you can say, "I love You, Lord, and adore You, and worship You," and still feel you are not saying everything you want to say, even though you do not know exactly what else to say. When you pray in the spirit, you can say everything. This makes your time of prayer and worship all the more intimate, special, and relevant.

Helping in Our Weaknesses

One other important benefit of speaking with tongues is found in Romans 8:26. Paul starts out in that verse by saying, **Likewise the Spirit also helps in our weaknesses. For we do not know what we should pray for as we ought....** Many people misquote this verse, and say, "You know, the Bible says we don't know **how** to pray, so we need to do thus-and-so." This is not what Paul is saying.

Paul is saying that we do not always know what to pray for *as we ought*. This applies only to intercessory prayer, where your total prayer is on the behalf of, and for the benefit of, someone else. You can make general intercession, such as praying for leaders and other people in authority. But sometimes, you can be led to intercede more deeply, beyond your actual knowledge of the facts. All you know on the inside of you is that you have to pray. This is where, as Paul phrases it in the latter part of Romans 8:26, **... the Spirit Himself makes intercession for us with groanings which cannot be uttered.**

The essence of what Paul writes here, in the original Greek, is that the groanings made by the Holy Spirit cannot be uttered in articulate speech. Again, this is because our native vocabulary runs out, and there is nothing else we can say. But when we pray with other tongues, we can say everything that needs to be said.

God has put no superfluous things in the Body of Christ. If He gave it, He gave it for a purpose. When it comes to speaking with tongues, we should certainly take the time to investigate it scripturally. We should be willing to reap the benefits God accrues to us through tongues, without any fear, prejudice, or misconception.

Reference Scriptures

The Holy Spirit

Genesis 1:1-3, 26	John 17:7-8, 13
Genesis 5:2	Acts 5:1-4
Genesis 6:3	Acts 7:51
Psalm 139:7-10	Acts 16:6-7
Isaiah 63:10	Romans 8:11, 26-27
John 3:5-6	Romans 15:16
Matthew 12:31-32	1 Corinthians 2:9-10
John 14:26	1 Thessalonians 5:19
John 15:26	Hebrews 9:14

Scriptures on Receiving the Holy Spirit

John 14:16-17	Acts 8:14-21
John 14:26	Acts 9:17-18
Luke 11:9-13	Acts 11:15-18
John 7:37-39	Acts 19:1-6
Acts 1:8	1 Corinthians 14:2,
Acts 2:1-4, 38-39	14-15, 18

Reference Scriptures
(continued)

Gifts of the Spirit

1 Corinthians 12:1-14

Fruit of the Spirit

Galatians 5:22-23

3

Building on a Firm
Foundation —
The Principles of Faith

**Death and life are in the power of the
tongue,
And those who love it will eat its fruit.**

Proverbs 18:21 informs us of a spiritual
law that few Christians have a grasp on. Yet,
this verse is perhaps one of the most awesome
scriptures in the Bible. Its implication is stag-
gering. God has put whether we succeed or
fail in life into our own hands through the
words of our mouths. We have the authority
to speak life and success, or death and defeat
to our lives. It's all up to us!

As Christians, we should be believing and
confessing the Word of God over every circumstance if we are to be successful in life. But

29

in addition to understanding this fact, understanding the other basic facts of faith are likewise essential. If you are going to walk by faith, you need to know these principles and get them into your spirit. This way, you can truly build your Christian walk on a firmer foundation.

Principle #1 — Faith Is a Way of Life

One of the first rules you have to understand about faith is that it is not a "get-what-I-want" plan. Romans 1:17 tells us that **"The just shall live by faith."** Faith (believing and acting on God's Word — the Bible) should be a way of life for every Believer, primarily because it pleases God (Hebrews 11:6).

Certainly, when we are doing all we can to please our heavenly Father, we can anticipate that He will do what He says He will do in His Word. This is especially true since Psalm 138:2 tells us that God has magnified His Word above His name. Therefore, we can have the utmost confidence in the Lord and in His willingness to act on our behalf.

However, because there are spiritual forces surrounding us that are continuously attempting to make God's Word ineffective in our lives, the manifestation of what we have prayed for and are believing God for may take some time. It is what we say and how we act during the time that we are standing in faith that gives impetus to our faith for either victory or defeat.

According to Romans 12:3 in the King James Version of the Bible, every Believer, upon becoming born again, is dealt the measure of faith. In other words, each person is given the same measure or amount of faith. However, it is up to the individual to develop this faith into a viable force.

Principle #2 —
Our Lifestyle MUST Coincide with God's Word

Faith comes by repeatedly hearing the Word of God (Romans 10:17), and is developed by putting the Word into action. Nevertheless, for your faith to work effectively on your behalf, you must make sure that you are living in line with the Bible to the best of your ability. You must have no strife in your heart against anyone. This would include any repressed anger, hatred, unforgiveness, resentment, or envy. Such an attitude can short-circuit your faith and thereby hinder you from receiving God's promised blessings to the fullest. You must also be living a moral and holy lifestyle in keeping with Bible doctrine. You should also have a daily time of prayer and study of the Word in communion with your heavenly Father.

If you are to become strong in faith, praying in the Spirit consistently is a MUST. Jude 20 tells us that we build our "spirit man" up on our most holy faith by praying in the Holy Spirit — that is, by praying or speaking with other tongues according to Acts 2:4.

Another important facet of Christianity is water baptism. Every individual, upon becoming born again, should be baptized in water. While water baptism is not a requisite for being saved, it is a biblical admonishment (Acts 10:47).

Principle #3 —
Faith Continually Grows

To grow in faith is a process. For example, we cannot expect our faith to produce $5,000 if it has not been successful in producing $5. Faith is also a spiritual force. It takes considerably more force to move a mountain than it does to move a molehill.

Many people do not comprehend these two aspects of faith, which work together to bring forth whatever the person is standing in faith to manifest. Oftentimes, if the situation is serious or life-threatening (as in the case of believing for a physical healing), there may not be enough faith force built up in a person to override the onslaught of the enemy. This is where the power of agreement can be effective. If a person's faith alone is not strong enough to bring about what is desired, God has instituted the spiritual law of agreement, which allows the combined faith of two or more people to produce results.

It takes time for faith to develop, because it only grows as it is exercised. As with a farmer

33

who plants a corn seed, there is a time span for that seed to grow into a full stalk of corn. The farmer first plants the seed, then he tends it by watering and caring for the seed. When the plant comes up, the farmer continues to tend and care for the plant until it grows into a full stalk of corn, and a harvest of an ear of corn is forthcoming.

Faith is like that corn seed. The faith seed is watered and cared for by our continually confessing, acting on, believing, and meditating on the Word. As we remain steadfast in doing these things, an image of what we are using our faith for should become a part of us, living within our spirits — then the harvest comes.

Principle #4 —
God Always Honors His Word

Another important rule of faith is that we cannot act first and then expect God to come in line with our actions. God will come in line with His Word if we are acting on it (Mark 16:20). To act on a desire or even to act on what we think is the right thing to do at the time will not necessarily move the hand of God. What will move His hand and still the enemy of mankind, Satan (the cause of sickness, sin, and evil in the world), is our acting in faith — a faith immovable and steadily increasing by a developing trust and confidence in God. We can grow to this level of faith as we put the Word into action, receive, and then grow from faith to faith by each successful culmination of what we have used our faith to produce.

It is not how good we are, or what we are doing for the Lord, or even how much we love the Lord — all of these will receive their just rewards (1 Corinthians 3:13-15). But if we want earthly prosperity, we must believe, act, and confess the Word.

Principle #5 —
Faith Is Not Moved by the
Circumstances

Not looking at the circumstances means you are not moved by the negative situations confronting you. Take healing for an example. When you are believing for your healing, you are not moved by what the doctors say. You are not moved by how you feel or how you look. You don't get depressed and start confessing all the negative things concerning your condition. You only look at what God has said or promised in the Bible about your condition.

The Bible says that with Jesus' stripes you were healed (1 Peter 2:24). This is what you keep your mind on, and not on what the doctors or the circumstances say. I am sure you can see that one would have to be a very disciplined person to act this way. You develop this discipline by an act of your will and a determination to do God's Word.

If you have any doubt as to your ability or willingness to operate in faith, or there is self-condemnation because of a particular lifestyle, then the services of a good doctor, lawyer, counselor, loan officer, or whatever, can be a beneficial resource.

Principle #6 —
Faith Operates at Various Levels

There are levels to faith. The highest level is to take God at His Word and to stand on that Word until the manifestation of what you are believing for occurs. If you do not have enough time to develop your faith to this level without endangering your life or worsening the situation, then you should utilize whatever solution is lawfully or medically available along with faith.

You can and should always be using your faith on something. Begin to believe God, no matter where you are spiritually. Make a determination to develop your faith by continually exercising it until it becomes like the seed that grows into a tree (Matthew 13:31-32). The more you exercise your faith, the more easily you will overcome any challenge the enemy throws at you, and you can keep on walking without so much as breaking stride.

Reference Scriptures

James 2:20	Proverbs 3:5-6
1 Timothy 1:5	1 Timothy 1:9
1 Timothy 1:19	James 1:6-7
James 2:5	James 2:22
Acts 6:5	Mark 11:23-24
Romans 10:17	Hebrews 11:1, 6
Romans 12:3	Matthew 8:5-10
Matthew 14:22-31	Romans 4:17-21
1 John 5:4	2 Thessalonians 1:3

4

Healing —
The Children's Bread
(Matthew 15:22-28)

If we were to take a poll of people from every denomination, we would probably have no argument from anyone on whether or not God can heal. I am sure the people polled would admit that God can heal any person of any physical condition if He wants to. But if this is truly the case, why then are so many Believers dying every day of sickness and disease?

For the sake of argument, let us say it is not God's will for every one of His blood-bought children to be healed. How do we find out, then, which people God wants to heal? To find the answer to this question, we would have to look at whom Jesus healed when He ministered in this earth-realm. Once we make this determination, we can use the same principle to ascertain whom God will heal today.

Matthew 8:16-17:

When evening had come, they brought to Him many who were demon-possessed. And He cast out the spirits with a word, and healed all who were sick, that it might be fulfilled which was spo ken by Isaiah the prophet, saying: "He Himself took our infirmities and bore our sicknesses."

Matthew 9:35:

Then Jesus went about all the cities and villages, teaching in their synagogues, preaching the gospel of the kingdom, and healing every sickness and every disease among the people.

Luke 6:17-19:

And He came down with them and stood on a level place with a crowd of His disciples and a great multitude of people from all Judea and Jerusalem, and from the seacoast of Tyre and Sidon, who came to hear Him and be healed of their disease, as well

as those who were tormented with unclean
spirits. And they were healed.

And the whole multitude sought to touch
Him, for power went out from Him and
healed them all.

In each of these passages, and in many others in the four Gospels, the pattern is the
same. Jesus healed everyone who wanted to
be healed. Let me also point out that every
one of the people Jesus healed was living
under the Old Covenant. Paul tells us in
Hebrews 8:6:

But now He [Jesus] has obtained a more
excellent ministry, inasmuch as He is also
Mediator of a better covenant, which was
established on better promises.

If the New Covenant is better than the Old
Covenant, our covenant should have all the
benefits afforded under the Old Covenant,
plus more. If this is the case, how could people under the Old Covenant be healed, and
people under the New Covenant — the "better covenant" — not be healed? This would
not make sense.

Why Everyone Is Not Healed Today

Many times, a person's opinion on divine healing is based on the experience of people, not on God's Word. For example, some "wonderful saint of God" was stricken with some sickness or disease, and the people in the church prayed for this person, but this person died anyway.

If you operate strictly in human understanding, it can be difficult to say that the person who died could have missed something. The conclusion is often made that the Lord "took" the person, and that it is not God's will for everyone to be healed.

I am not in any way trying to cast aspersions on the commitment or love of the saint who passed on, nor on that person's relationship with the Lord. However, if he or she did not know the truth concerning divine healing, that person was going to die unless he or she had a good doctor, or God intervened supernaturally through the gifts of the Spirit.

That person's dying had nothing to do with loving the Lord. It had to do with a spiritual law that is stated in Hosea 4:6: **My people are destroyed for lack of knowledge.** According to this law, if we have adequate, proper scriptural knowledge, this knowledge can stand between us and disaster.

Sometimes people go to a church and are prayed for, yet they do not get healed. This does not mean God does not want them healed. It can mean that the minister who is praying for those individuals may be praying in unbelief. This does not mean that the minister does not love the Lord. It may be that the minister simply does not know how to pray and what to do according to the Word. In Matthew 17, we have a perfect example of this situation.

Matthew 17:14-16:

And when they had come to the multitude, a man came to Him, kneeling down to Him and saying,

"Lord, have mercy on my son, for he is an epileptic and suffers severely; for he often falls into the fire and often into the water.

"So I brought him to Your disciples, but they could not cure him."

The statement the father makes in verse 16 tells us something. If the disciples could not cure the man's son, why did he waste his time bringing his son to someone who could not help him?

What happened is that the disciples *did not* cure the man's son. Because they *did not* heal him, the father concluded that they *could not* heal him. But there is a difference between *could not* and *did not*.

Matthew 17:17-19:

> **Then Jesus answered and said, "O faithless and perverse generation, how long shall I be with you? How long shall I bear with you? Bring him here to Me."**
>
> **And Jesus rebuked the demon, and it came out of him; and the child was cured from that very hour.**
>
> **Then the disciples came to Jesus privately and said, "Why could we not cast it out?"**

If the disciples did not have the ability or the authority, they would have known it. They came to Jesus and asked, "Why could we not cast it out?" The fact that they asked Him this question means they knew they could do it. For some reason, this time the power did not work, and they did not know why.

Unbelief — Then and Now

Notice how Jesus answered the disciples' question.

Matthew 17:19-20:

Then the disciples came to Jesus privately and said, "Why could we not cast it out?"
So Jesus said to them, "Because of your unbelief...."

You can just as easily have unbelief operating in the preacher, the pulpit, and the church. If you are operating in unbelief, God's power to heal will not work, even when it is the will of God for it to work!

This is exactly what has happened in many churches. Simply because sometimes a person was not healed, the minister has concluded that it was not God's will. He would never consider the possibility that he could be at fault, that it was possible that his faith was weak. He may not know any better because he has never been taught any better; and if he is not informed in God's Word, he cannot operate on what he does not know.

If it were really God's will not to heal everyone, what would we do with a verse like Matthew 8:17:

> **that it might be fulfilled which was spoken by Isaiah the prophet, saying:**
>
> **"He Himself took our infirmities and bore our sicknesses."**

Likewise, what would we do with 1 Peter 2:24:

> **who Himself bore our sins in His own body on the tree; that we, having died to sins, might live for righteousness — by whose stripes you were healed.**

When Jesus was taken into Pilate's judgment hall, and the Roman soldiers laid 39 stripes upon His back with a whip, God saw every disease of mankind transferred to Jesus' body. When the soldiers had finished their scourging, they took Jesus to Calvary and nailed Him to a cross. When they killed Him, they also killed the sicknesses — and that made you free from sickness and disease. The verse reads, **by whose stripes you were healed.** If you were healed, that means you are healed, in the name of Jesus.

If healing were not for every Christian, what would we do with James 5:14-15:

> **Is anyone among you sick? Let him call for the elders of the church, and let them pray over him, anointing him with oil in the name of the Lord.**
>
> **And the prayer of faith will save the sick, and the Lord will raise him up. And if he has committed sins, he will be forgiven.**

According to these verses, the Lord will raise up anyone who is sick. I do not care how many people have prayed for you. If you are sick, you have a right to be well. If you are not prayed for rightly, you may not get healed. But by the same token, Jesus promises us in the latter part of Matthew 17:20:

> **"... for assuredly, I say to you, if you have faith as a mustard seed, you will say to this**

mountain, 'Move from here to there,' and it will move; and nothing will be impossible for you."

If you have the boldness to take God at His Word, to ask Him in faith for your healing, and to stand in faith until that healing physically manifests, no matter how long it takes, you will be healed.

Divine healing is for every Christian. If you are not walking in divine health, you are not only going against the will of God, but you are walking far below the privileges that Jesus gave His life for you to have. It does not mean you are not a Christian, or that you do not love God. It just means that you are living below the privileges Jesus has provided for you.

Take advantage of the best God has made available for your life. You can live above the circumstances of defeat, including sickness and disease. Healing is for all — have no doubt about it!

Reference Scriptures

Matthew 8:17	Luke 13:11-16
Mark 16:17-18	1 Peter 2:24
Acts 19:11-12	Matthew 15:29-31
Matthew 9:1-8	Acts 3:1-10
Mark 11:24	3 John 2
Acts 10:38	Mark 5:24-34
Matthew 9:27-30	

5

Tithes and Offerings — God's Financial Plan

In John 10:10, Jesus says that He came so that we might have life and have it more abundantly. It goes without saying that the Believer who desires to enjoy the abundant life in Christ Jesus, and secure both the blessings of Abraham and those promised in Deuteronomy 28, must be living a lifestyle that is in line with the principles established in the Word of God. Living right is a prerequisite to receiving any of the blessings of God.

In Malachi 3:8, God asks:

> **"Will a man rob God?**
> **Yet you have robbed Me!**
> **But you say,**
> **'In what way have we robbed You?'**
> [And God answers] **'In tithes and**
> **offerings.'"**

Based on this verse, if you are not a tither, you are a God-robber. I robbed God for years, and as a result, I was actually robbing myself! So I am glad that I can now say "I am not a God-robber." I was the one getting cheated because God is still God, whether I give Him anything or not.

Notice that it is God who is asking the question, **"Will a man rob God?"** Of course, He already knows the answer and He anticipates your inquiry as to how you may have robbed Him. **"In tithes and offerings,"** He responds. And for this reason, God says that **"You are cursed with a curse"** (Malachi 3:9).

Whether you know about this curse or not, it is still loose in the earth-realm and operating in the lives of those who do not participate in God's financial plan of prosperity through the giving of tithes and offerings. There are multitudes of people operating in this curse without even knowing it. As I mentioned, I operated in this curse for years and did not know it. It just seemed that no matter how much money I earned, there simply was not enough to meet the needs of my family and myself. I thought this was a reality of my life — the color of my skin — not the result of operating under a curse.

Thank God that in His financial plan there is always enough, for He is El Shaddai — the God of more than enough. He is Jehovah-jireh, your Provider — provided you follow His plan. His desire is that you prosper, so His method of tithes and offerings incorporates a reciprocal relationship. The moment you give to God, your heavenly Father gives back to you! However, there is a time element involved. God is in the spirit world and that spirit world is outside the realm of the physical. The blessings God has given us as the result of our giving have to come from the spirit world into the physical world and it is faith that makes this transfer.

Meanwhile, Satan is waiting between these two worlds to steal your blessings as they are sent by God. He is ever poised and ready. He comes to kill, steal, and destroy (John 10:10). The only way you can keep his hands off of your blessings is by using your faith. You have to be confessing the

Word and saying, "In the name of Jesus, I believe I receive the windows of heaven blessing."

Each time you proclaim this confession, while walking in line with God's principles, you make inroads into the spirit-realm and bring your blessings forth from the spirit world into the physical world. When you systematically continue to make your confessions relative to your tithes and offerings, Satan cannot touch your blessings. But when you fail to adhere to the directives given in God's Word, Satan can and will steal your blessings and there is nothing God can do about it.

Where Is The Storehouse?

Another important factor to understand about tithing is where the storehouse is located. Malachi 3:10 directs us to:

> **"Bring all the tithes into the storehouse,**
> **That there may be food in My house,**
> **And try Me now in this,"**

> Says the LORD of hosts,
> "If I will not open for you the windows
>   of heaven,
> And pour out for you such blessing
> That there will not be room enough to
>   receive it."

The tithe is considered 10 percent of your net income — whether that income is from your job, rental property, unemployment benefits, stocks and bonds, or a retirement fund. Whatever your income, your tithe is 10 percent of what you actually have to live on, exclusive of taxes and other payroll deductions.

Of course, a savings plan does not fall into your gross earnings, but into your net earnings. In other words, if you have a savings plan where deductions are automatically made from your payroll check before you get it, this sum is still a part of your net earnings and should be included in the amount from which you compute your tithes, with the exception of a retirement savings program, etc. Tithing should begin from the program when monies from the program become your income.

The storehouse is where you are being taught how to apply God's Word to every circumstance in your life. This should be the church where you worship and fellowship with the saints. Notice that I said, "where you are being taught." Only you know where you are being fed the Word of God, so where you consider your storehouse to be is your decision. Just remember that you will have to give an account to the Lord as to where you place your tithes. So you want to be sure that your tithes and offerings are always "planted in good ground."

Seed-time and Harvest

There is a time frame from the time you begin tithing and giving offerings until the blessings begin showing up. I believe the following illustration will help you better understand the principles of seed-time and harvest.

Obviously, you cannot plant a seed one morning and expect to reap a harvest that same evening. Seeds simply do not grow that fast. But the moment you plant good seed into good ground, the germination process begins. When the elements within the seed and the soil begin to interact, germination immediately starts. Now, you cannot see this process because it is taking place under ground; nonetheless, germination is in effect.

When you go to water your seed a few days or weeks later, you will notice that the earth is cracked in the area where you planted your seed. The next time you go to tend to your seed, you will notice that the crack is even a little wider. Within the next few days or so, you might even see a little green blade coming up. In the coming weeks, that little blade will get bigger and bigger until finally you will be able to see a plant coming up out of the ground.

When you first saw this green blade above the ground is not when the seed you planted actually started growing. Your seed was growing all the time, but the ground prohibited you from seeing your seed's growth. This is why it is so important to maintain your confession of "I believe I receive." In the spirit world, such a confession keeps your seed (whatever you are believing and confessing) growing.

Unfortunately, some people become discouraged when they do not see the manifestation of their desire right away. They stop tithing and confessing the windows of heaven blessing. You do not want to be tricked into thinking, "Well, that is really something! I planted my seed seven days ago, and I do not see anything yet. I'll just go ahead and plow this ground up, pour some concrete, and make a patio instead." If you do this, you will end up missing your blessings.

In the natural, you have learned to have confidence that the seed you plant will grow once you plant them into the ground, even though you cannot see that growth taking place. Your physical eyes cannot penetrate the ground to witness their growth. Nevertheless, you keep right on watering your seed, believing eventually you will see the results.

This same principle applies to spiritual blessings. You cannot see into the spirit world, just as you cannot see into the physical ground. Nonetheless, you have to believe that this process is working all the time. Since you believe God is going to pour you out a blessing, you should have your baskets ready to receive. You have to do this by faith, or the devil will steal what rightfully belongs to you. When you have your faith in operation for your desire, you can then have confidence that Satan cannot steal what belongs to you because of what God promises in Malachi 3:11:

> **"And I will rebuke the devourer for your sakes,**
> **So that he will not destroy the fruit of your ground,**
> **Nor shall the vine fail to bear fruit for you in the field,"**
> **Says the LORD of hosts.**

God's Provisions

Once I found out how to tap into the provisions God has made available for the Body of Christ, I was able to get from under the curse that had plagued me a great part of my adult life. Before learning how to operate in God's financial plan, my wife and I never had enough money to take care of our material needs. In fact, I was barely able to provide the necessities of life for my family.

This is why, when I heard about faith, I completely sold out to doing things God's way. My wife and I certainly could not have become any worse off than we already were! Once I discovered that my prosperity was through tithing and the giving of offerings, I made up my mind that I was going to tithe. Thank God no one could tell me anything different from God's Word about tithing because today my family is reaping the benefits from my decision not to be a God-robber.

A certain insurance company uses an open umbrella with raindrops falling around it as its trademark. Rain is falling on and all around the umbrella, but under the umbrella it is dry. This image portrays the concept that protection from financial calamity is provided through this company's insurance coverage — the rain being the calamity and the umbrella being the protection.

This same analogy applies to God's financial plan. The rain is like the curse of the law listed in Deuteronomy 28:15-68. This curse is all around you, like the rain falling from the sky. But under the umbrella of God's Word, you are safe, dry, and secure. The umbrella does not stop the rain from falling, but it does stop the rain from falling on you.

Years ago, I began hoisting my umbrella of protection by putting faith and tithing into operation in my life. I began to tithe and to confess the return on my tithes and offerings. It was a while before I saw any appreciable change. It takes time for faith to grow to the point where you start receiving fruit from the seed you have planted in the Kingdom of God through tithes and offerings, and watered by your consistent positive confession. But every day I would thank God for the windows of heaven blessing, confessing that I believed I had received as God had promised in His Word.

I tell you that once you get on a roll, the blessings of God seem to just keep coming in until you become, as the Bible says, exceedingly abundantly blessed! Not only are your own needs well-supplied, but more importantly, you are able to contribute substantially to the work of getting the Gospel to a dying and needy world while still having plenty to be a blessing to others in need.

Twenty-Percent Penalty

If you should ever consider "borrowing" from the tithe, or should just stop tithing altogether because of some pressing financial need, with the intention of tithing again when the situation is resolved, remember that there is a penalty for doing so:

Leviticus 27:30-31:

> **'And all the tithe of the land, whether of the seed of the land or of the fruit of the tree, is the LORD'S. It is holy to the LORD.**
> **'If a man wants at all to redeem any of his tithes, he shall add one-fifth [or 20 percent] to it.'**

Once I was a chief exponent of "borrowing" from the tithe. I did not realize I was again being a God-robber. I figured I could get away with it. But as soon as I started cutting back on my tithes, the umbrella of God's protection folded up, and I was again operating under the curse. I did not even know it! At first, I could not figure out what was wrong and why I was having such a hard time of it. Then I found out what was going on, and I got my act together. Now I tithe 25% of all my income, plus give offerings. I do not ever intend for that mess to happen to me again!

I started out tithing the required 10 percent of my net income. I increased my tithe to 12.5%, then to 15%, and now I am at 25% of my net income. I give a quarter out of every dollar I receive as income. I believe that one day I will be in a position to tithe 50% of my income. I can say this with all honesty and sincerity because I have learned the great benefits of God's financial plan and His way of prosperity. My desire is that you, too, will reap the harvest as you continue to sow into God's plan of prosperity.

Reference Scriptures

John 10:10   Matthew 7:7
Psalm 34:10   Matthew 8:18
Proverbs 3:9-10   Matthew 6:33
Proverbs 8:20-21   Genesis 24:31-32
3 John 2   Galatians 3:13-14
Deuteronomy 8:18   Malachi 3:8-11
Deuteronomy 28:1-8   Leviticus 27:30-31
Luke 6:38   Philippians 4:19
2 Corinthians 9:6

About the Author

Apostle Frederick K.C. Price is the founder of Crenshaw Christian Center in Los Angeles, California, and Crenshaw Christian Center East in Manhattan, New York. He is known worldwide as a teacher of the biblical principles of faith, healing, prosperity and the Holy Spirit. During his more than 50 years in ministry, countless lives have been changed by his dynamic and insightful teachings that truly "tell it like it is."

His television program, Ever Increasing Faith Ministries (EIFM), has been broadcast throughout the world for more than 25 years and currently airs in 15 of the 20 largest markets in America, reaching an audience of more than 15 million households each week. EIFM is also webcast on the Internet via www.faithdome.org. The EIFM radio program is heard on stations across the world, including the continent of Europe via short-wave radio.

In addition, in 1990, Apostle Price founded the Fellowship of Inner City Word of Faith Ministries (FICWFM, which has since been renamed to the Fellowship of International Christian Word of Faith Ministries due to its growth and global reach,). Members of FICWFM include churches from all over the United States and various countries. The Fellowship, which meets regionally throughout the year and hosts an annual convention, is not a denomination. Their mission is to provide fellowship, leadership, guidance and a spiritual covering for those desiring a standard of excellence in ministry.

Apostle Price holds an honorary doctorate of divinity degree from Oral Roberts University and an honorary diploma from Rhema Bible Training Center.

Apostle Price is the author of some 50 books on faith, healing, prosperity, and the Holy Spirit. "How Faith Works" is a classic book on the operation of faith and its life-changing principles. He has sold over 2.1 million books since 1976. His most recent book projects include, "Prosperity: Good News for God's People" and "Answered Prayer Guaranteed: The Power of Praying with Faith."

To receive Dr. Price's book and tape catalog
or be placed on the EIF mailing list,
please call:

(800) 927-3436

*Books are also available
at local bookstores everywhere.*

For more information, please write:

**Crenshaw Christian Center
P.O. Box 90000
Los Angeles, CA 90009**

or check your local TV or Webcast listing:

Ever Increasing Faith Ministries

or visit our Website:

www.faithdome.org

500 0.00
30,000.00

2 Samel 9:1..........

1 Samuel 20:14-15

Rev. 3:20

Heb 5:14